*M*usings
in a pandemic
and beyond

reviews

The many losses of the 2020 pandemic have brought many of us to our knees, a place of both surrender and reverence. gloria fern shares evocative and poignant reflections from her perspective as mother, grandmother, environmentalist and poet. A worthwhile and nourishing series to help you through tough times.

— **Nancy Leach**, *author of the Mindful Bloomer:*
Skills for Living and Dying, mindfulbloomer.ca

The Muse was clearly sitting close by gloria as she penned the lovely poems for this heartfelt collection. From sparse verse to rich imagery, these poems drawn from nature, family, memory and desire are a tribute to the role that poetry can-and should-play in challenging times. Musings captures the achingly poignant "normal' we need to celebrate and create every day.

— **Day Merrill**, *Poet Laureate Emeritus*
Town of Collingwood, Ontario

Musings
in a pandemic and beyond

gloria fern

Copyright © 2020 Gloria Nafziger

All rights reserved. No part of this publication may be reproduced or transmitted in any form or by any means, electronic or mechanical, including photocopying, recording, or any information storage and retrieval system, without permission in writing from the author.

Published in 2020 by
Kinetics Design, KDbooks.ca
ISBN 978-1-988360-44-7 (paperback)
ISBN 978-1-988360-45-4 (ebook)

Photographs by Theo Siemens-Rhodes

Cover and interior design, typesetting and printing by Daniel Crack,
Kinetics Design, KDbooks.ca
www.linkedin.com/in/kdbooks/

Contact the author at
gfern52@gmail.com

Musings is dedicated to

Aunt Reta

My pandemic musings

Introduction	9
In a Moment	11
Black Currants	12
April Weeps	13
Pansies	14
True or Just Real	15
Unite	16
Present Absence	18
Full Moon	19
Defeating	20
The Edge	22
Triplets	23
Love in the Time of Covid-19	25
Normal	27
Good Friday	28
Covid-19: An Invitation	30
Easter Morn	32
Life Cycles	33

Instinct	35
Apndemic	36
Oft Shrouded	38
Teeter Totter	39
Sunday	41
Lockdown	42
Grieving in the Spring of 2020	43
Forget Me Not	44
Another Pandemic Day	45
Seventeen	46
Six or Seven or Eight	48
Dysania	49
S A F E ?	51
Tanya and Galia	52
Borrowed Bones	53
We Rise Again	54
In a Moment	57
Acknowledgments	59

Introduction

I did not imagine a global pandemic lasting over nine months when I began writing these poems. I thought, I really believed, I was writing poems for others, for you. As the months of pandemic have continued, I have come to realize more and more that the poems were written for me, to sustain me. These poems offered me companionship in my times of isolation, they accompanied me through loneliness. They have brought comfort in the midst of unpredictability.

I share them now with the belief that they can bring hope.

There is a part of me that still believes, oh these so many weeks after I wrote the first poem in this collection, that this pandemic gives us a chance for redemption. A chance to become the wonderful people we are meant to be.

These poems are an invitation for you to find hope, to see possibility in the midst of these most impossible of times. May the poems here offer you inspiration for noticing the light that is present in the actions of so many people. My invitation to you, and to me, is to submit to the possibilities of the good visible in the new realities of these days while at the same time releasing our desire to resist.

gloria fern

In a Moment

everything can change . . .

Live life,

love all peoples

today.

Black Currants

Sourdough bread slathered in black currant jam, from
    last summer's loaded bushes
    harvested, washed, made into jam when the idea
    that there would be NO flour in the grocery store
        every
        time
        we went
        was an absurdity.

A bike ride with a friend
      six feet   apart
    and we so fortunate as to
    have trails almost empty, and spring
    peepers to welcome us in the marshy
    corner of a gravel trail.

Crunchy stop.

Bullfrogs call notice
    pussy willows and forsythia budding forth,
    cardinals, chickadees dance,
    spirit companions on our journey.

Dinner offers stew rich with the wonder of tomatoes found in the depth
    of our chest-freezer, cleaned in these long, strange pandemic days
    waiting spring sap offerings, summer harvest,
    and in July,
    more currants — hope's gift today.

April Weeps

Tears like raindrops fall
forty days of making music
giving gratitude for essential workers
forty days I have been sheltering
in place with people who love me
forty days I have watched
the news with hope, with despair
forty days have passed
since I held a grandchild in my arms
forty days of hope
of believing we could
make it end, this nightmare
called pandemic
today the sky snivels
joins me in deep longing
blooms, bright yellow
reflect droplets of sorrow.

May day, mayday
come now Beltane's eve

    I seek
        release.

Pansies

Still blooming surprises
    of purple, yellow and blue
spindles of growth continue
    in spite of the cool

Rains, hail, bouncing on soil.
    shivering in the dawn
    beaten and worn

They lift
    wearied heads.

True or Just Real

with thanks to Carrie Newcomer for her poetic gems

"Is it true or just real?"
    that line in Carrie's poem
    invades me these days
    invades my thoughts
    as i (small i) remember the years of
    my life, the ones that got me to here
    past the time when
    i knew old age had hit.

    i have known so many
    truths in these years
    and they have changed
    become reality that I (capital I) live by
    sometimes, that I hold onto.

They have blown away
    with the wind, a gust grabbing hold
    just when I least expected it and
    a new reality becomes as clear as real
    as the last one I knew
    with the certainty that
    spring will come, the green heads pushing up where
    snow lay, will lead to new blooms
    and leaves and shoots
    and they will be real
    and truthful too?

Unite

The sky like, my soul, is weeping
    grey dreariness covers the sun
    hiding, it seems, from
    crocus's passionate bloom
    daffodils wrapped in scarves
    mittens still on
    tulips pushing forward.

These days of held breath
    watch
    hope
    as music plays.

Breaking hearts hears news of
    yet another seniors' home with deaths
    and loss of staff and residents
    other deaths — on pleasure destined
    cruises, no rescue yet for
    those on board.

We wait in prayer, in silent ritual,
    meditative, yoga stance, believing
    that our friend, will not test positive and
    that if they do, they will be saved
    the horrors of a death absent from
    hands held family or friend.

These days of love and caring
    sent across the wires, connection felt.

The sun breaks through
    in you.

Present Absence

You lived, danced
> amidst flowers
> in waves, laughter
> filled your outrage.

Death came
> tears fell
> your body burned,
> ashes flew

You dance
> with the birds
> in the waves
> with the flowers

Full
Moon

Bright red tulips

trillium buds,
238 days left
in this year.

Snowflakes

the size of pancakes
fall amidst
candles lit, reused wax
reforming hope.

Defeating

Two boys play happily
  ninja warriors defeat the bad guys
  always.

I walk, with a smile, into
  the grocery store, on the street
  talk across the six-foot barrier.

Deep gratitude for
  leaders, for a social network,
  for medical professionals.

Concern for friends and family
  hopeful for a world, for growing
  consciousness.

Delight in technology's gifts
  for scavenger hunts, photos posted
  in three cities, in two countries,
  for musicians, craft ideas
  and so many untried recipes
  for artists doing tutorials, and
  the call to meditate, the
  call to slow down, to be aware, to
  focus on world peace, on
  love.

Grieve with those who grieve,
   laugh with those who laugh,
   hold one another in spirit.

Grateful for health care workers,
   for scientists, for researchers, for
   spiritual teachers.

Walk with gratitude for the
   sun, the wind, the water, the trees,
   the buds, the bulbs sprouting.

Two knights play happily
   now, defeating dragons.

The Edge

*Equinox has come
    and gone, along with
    grandchildren's laughter, visits
    on the edge of a pandemic
    barely visible.*

*My beloved has a sore
    throat, every morning,
    every night and sometimes
    throughout the day, I ask,*

Do you have a fever?

*On the edge of a pandemic
    barely visible.*

Triplets

Delight, despair, and desire combine forces

    as we drive down country lanes in search of
    adventure, seeking something

    they stumble through the ditch
    unto the road barely

    noticing
    our car, almost upon them

    while a doe, their mother,
    watches anxiously, silencing fears
    offering gentle nuzzles of
    love.

Love in the
Time of Covid-19

I awaken, rub sleep dust from my eyes, sun
   streaming in through the windows, dog
   scratching on doors, sourdough
   bread smells wafting through the house.

I wander in the garden, so fortunate to have one, see
   crocuses blooming forth, daffodils budding, tulip leaves, and
   along our walk —
   water rushing across the path.

Waves lap on the shore, on the big water, and did I mention
   my good fortune? Friends wave across the six-foot
   mile, bagpipes echo forth around the world. Scotland
   the Brave in my front yard.

The sidewalk chalk, the seeds harvested and shared, the beef stew
   with meat from local farmers' fields. Not like mother made
   but robust with red wine. Laundry blowing
   on the line, cool winds, sky
   blue.

Someone found me and asked me
   to be her friend too,

               L o v e   c a l l e d   m e . . .

Normal

*I celebrate the normal of loving friends, smiling
    at strangers, greeting those we
    meet on our path, making space for all.*

*I celebrate the normal of Zoom, Skype, Facetime,
    with family and friends when their faces have
    been too long absent, physically.*

*I celebrate the normal of gratitude shared with
    grocery store clerks, garbage collectors, first responders,
    health care providers, and especially PSWs.*

*I celebrate the normal of neighbours gathering, sharing
    smiles, food, music; waving from
    the other end of the street just to say "Hi!"*

*I celebrate the normal of noticing our fossil fuel
    usage, of being conscious of Mother Earth and all her
    creatures, and clean air.*

*I celebrate the normal of blowing bubbles, sidewalk
    chalk messages of love, laughter, hope, hearts and
    rainbows brightening lives.*

*I celebrate the new normal of caring, of
    sharing, of generosity of daring to
    reach across difference.*

*I celebrate the normal of notes sent by mail,
    by email, of remembering, of time taken to
    let another know we care.*

*I celebrate the normal of seeing, smelling, feeling,
    of sunsets, and moon cycles of
    raindrops and budding trees.*

I celebrate the new normal we are noticing and creating.

Good Friday

I have always wondered why it was called 'Good,' —
  this Friday that falls somewhere around Eostre
  sometime close to Passover, and this year almost
  overlapping with Vaisakhi and Buddha day,
  — always in Christian tradition two days before Easter.

Easter, that celebration of new life, of
  growth. Easter, that day that joins
  with the holidays of other traditions, celebrating
  enlightenment, and freedom from slavery, and the
  new harvest. Those sacred holy days that call us to hope.

*I have always wondered why the day two days
    before, the day that Jesus is flogged, is crucified,
    dies: the curtain is torn, and sorrow is at its height —
    why is this day called GOOD?*

*I have read, have studied the theology: a holy day,
    a good day, and yet I have questioned,
today the question rests. I have felt resurrection in my life, over
    and over again.*

Today tulips are in bud.

*This is Good Friday,
    a day of grief, of loss, of confronting
    a father on a ventilator,
    an aunt in intensive care, no visitors allowed
    an exchange student breathing constricted, waiting …*

*There is no resurrection, no enlightenment, no new life,
no freedom from our enslavement called COVID-19 in sight,*

    *I sit believing this is not good, and yet the bulbs
    are budding, the generosity is visible, the compassion
    is growing.*

    Today is a good and holy day.

Covid-19: An Invitation

*I am invited by COVID-19 to show a little more
    appreciation for sunshine, health care, for caring
    government.*

*I am invited by COVID-19, to respect distance, to notice
    connection
    across distance and difference.*

*I am invited by COVID-19 to grieve for the many who
    grieve in Italy, in China,
    in Syria, in South Sudan:
    in this world we all share.*

*I am invited by COVID-19 to laugh with Pluto the dog,
    with memes,
    with grandchildren telling nonsensical jokes ...*

*I am invited by COVID-19 to reconsider my footprint on
    Mother Earth, to consider how I will live differently
    when COVID-19 has left my daily thoughts?*

*I am invited by COVID-19 to think a little more about
   my neighbours, those I know
   and those who remain strangers to me.*

*I am invited by COVID-19 to love the earth, the
   global family of which I and you are all a part.*

*I am invited by COVID-19 to be
   more compassionate.*

Easter Morn

It came peeking out of the clouds
    just a sliver of the sun,
    it was 6:41, bicycle wheels
    raced to get us there
    on time, after debate about cold, about rain
    through morning's musky scent
    eyes seeking
    speeding forward, needing perhaps
    to witness the sun rise
    to ensure it would happen
    on this most peculiar of Sunday mornings
    and it rose, there was shade
    there were clouds,
    but we saw it, as I have seen it
    many Easter's before, we alone
    were at the terminals, no trumpet
    sound, no carols sung, and yet there
    was a rising,
        like the cinnamon buns,

We walked among the sprouting
    plants, the buds not yet
    fully present to all that is,
    like me, not fully present to feeling
    it all, not wanting to notice the

        sorrow, the emptiness.

Only here in this moment —
    life.

Life Cycles

Today my baby turns 36.
We buried her daddy this week.
Her baby will turn 3 next week.
I buried my daddy three years ago.

This month
> *so full of turnings, turnings*
> *memories of days of delight*
> *of days of sorrow,*
> *confusion and wonder*
> *time's passage,*
> *creeping along*
> *rapidly.*

My grandmother used to tell
> *me "time goes faster when you are older."*
> *my wise young self, retorting*
"Grandma that doesn't make sense."

Sense making or not,
> *grandma was right, life passes:*
> *birth*
>> *then living*
>> *then death*

> *is how it goes.*

I am in the living now.

Instinct

These days of beauty and sorrow

of joy and fear, of

absence and connections, of

surety and doubt

as though the universe

were active

today,

a time of presence.

Apndemic

with thanks to Mary Oliver

*After your arrival
I jumped up and down,
I clapped my hands and
I stared into space.*

I walked toward the first warm sting of possibility

*In those days I was hungry for emptiness,
    go ahead tell me I was both silly and serious
    as my stomach groaned for the
    improbable possibility of days
    without demand or calendars.*

On the first day despite
> *national and international news*

I heard only the music from balconies,
> *the violinists, the soloists,*
> *the gratitude from empty streets.*

My imagination did not stretch
> *like the birds in flight overhead*
> *its range did not enter my heart now emptied*
> *of curly cuddles, it could not extend to*
> *the frozen terrain of my longing.*

After your arrival
> *I jumped up and down,*
> *I clapped my hands,*
> *I stared into space.*

Oft Shrouded

Have I ever told you?

Have I told you how much I like stories
 how they fuel me, inform me, and make me
 feel whole.

The stories I read see and hear,
 the costumes, the dancing, the song
 characters, like me and so different
 as well, the truth, the real
 the absurd.

I like movement and bodies;
 performance and risk,

They lead me from
 fear and
 uncertainty, away
 from obsession and grief.

They take me right there
 then back here.

Have I ever told you how much I like
 the curious sharing, the daring
 and caring

 the risk?

Teeter Totter

Hearts in windows, flowers on tables
    still blooming to those who mother
    and grandmother with gratitude and love,
    wind on the backs of the littles who know
    how to maintain distance connection
    without contradiction.

My sister-in-law graduated yesterday
    photos sent in time and space, and
    a grandson's graduation ceremony
    on Wednesday, we will be able
    to attend without eight hours of travel.

Oh, bitter joy.

"Hope is the expectation of future joy," says
    a sign in the window on this day
    of May, showers drizzling down on me,
    on our dog, on the freshly planted
    seedlings smiling from the squirrel-turned soil.

Sunday

Chickadees dance in treetops,
    branches bud filled,

Daffodils fill ditches,
    swans on nests, egrets
    wait
    wait
    wait for the moment
    like the fisherpeople
    rod holders displaced
    by deeply eroded shorelines

Our garden waits for seedlings,
    killdeer call, childhood returns to me
    the turned fields
    calves found next to mama, the baby chicks
    gaining feathers

    the feeder outside my kitchen
    window sways.

Lockdown

Moon covered by clouds

       frost covering buds

  children

gone wild after 8000 days

      or is it hours?

    Lockdown . . .

Grieving in the Spring of 2020

I have been sorting in these days of transition.
I have been sorting difference
    and sorting papers:
        Letters from my mother, from when I was in College in Virginia,
        letters from my boyfriend, filled with dreams of youth
        letters from my no-longer husband
        letters of love, of discouragement of hope, anger and joy.

The letters from my no-longer husband, the father of my children,
    he died this year
    before the arrival of a pandemic
    led me to sorting and discarding
    filling a box for shredding with memories good and not.

I am filled with gratitude for the love we shared.
Ron and I
For the children that were born of that love and
    the grandchildren,
    who, with his children,
    grieve his death.

I am filled with gratitude for the life I have chosen to live
    and for those who have walked with me on my path,
    and those who have joined me.

My children and grandchildren: the greatest gifts,
    and already in these early pandemic days I long for them.

Despite the distance that separates us, and
    the knowledge that we would not be physically together
    today even if
    this pandemic had not struck,

I miss them.
    Oh, how I miss them …

Forget Me Not

Clouds cover the sky

    dampness covers
    gardens, newly planted
    dug up again
    by them, those
    fluffy tailed rodents,
    photographed, with delight
    by those not from here,
    who are not gardeners.

The ants, they build
    their hills.

Diatomaceous earth
    sprinkled again mid
    petrichor, that earthy scent
    after the rain.

Bees cover the blossoms.

Permissible pleasure
    on purples and blues.

Another Pandemic Day

a.n.o.t.h.e.r.   day

a not her day

an other day

an other   d.a.y.

another day . . .

Seventeen

I miss his hugs, his smile
  which shines across the
screen

We sing a Tom Chapin's
  birthday song for him

Where did that song come from?
  asks our musician grandson.

My hope grows.

Six or Seven or Eight

Giddy excitement filled me
   as I prepared for
   six or seven or eight feet apart
   art shared with elaborate story
   six or seven or eight feet apart
   smell the bottoms of the fritillaria
   six or seven or eight feet apart
   children kneel on the ground
   six or seven or eight feet apart
   smelling skunks in plants
   six or seven or eight feet apart
   examine seeds, and create mud puddles
   six or seven or eight feet apart
   games (newly acquired) shown and explained,
   six or seven or eight feet apart
   watch the agility of climbers
   six or seven or eight feet apart
   the swing, the slide to slide to slide race
   six or seven or eight feet apart
   climbing hills, laughing,
   six or seven or eight feet apart
   you and
                yours and
                your presence
      felt
   and held
   six or seven or eight feet apart.

Dysania[1]

Another
black person
murdered

change

required
to furnish
hope

and yet another
black person
murdered

change

required to
polish hope

---

1 *to be unable to get out of bed*

SAFE?

Bees cover the currant bush
    orange, yellow, blue, red, like prayer flags[2]
    shredded.

Birds dance, dog poop
    everywhere, I think.

Stubbed toes, sourdough that did
    not rise today, soup too salty,
    or sweet. Or not.

Mud-covered, the children do not
    run towards me but play
    six feet away from a hug.

There will be no
    mud on me
    and now, there
    is rain.

---

2 Colourful Tibetan prayer flags are hung outdoors, filled with prayers, when they begin to shred/tear/disappear the prayers are said to be answered

Tanya and Galia

You asked me why

I sat among the shoes
    no piano room beauty
    but cubicles of shoes
    for inspiration.

I sat in hope

I sit in hope
    that shoes will come
    to lead my way.

I thought perhaps the right pair
    would climb down off the shelf

If I sat
    long enough
    the right ones
    would come
    and take me to my destination
    directly

No more circuitous routes
    on goat paths through mountains and ravines
    but directly
    to bliss, enlightenment, nirvana
    they have not yet come
    so
    still I sit
    and hope.

Borrowed Bones

Bones, sinus, flesh covered

Your sharing built
    their strength, my strength
      dead bones borrowed from a time before

      my mother's mother's mother's . . .
    inhabit me

    These borrowed bones.

We Rise Again

Cold winds blow,
*   snow, hail, sleet?*

Drums, dance,
*   bagpipes*
*   fiddle*

Rocks beauty painted
*   windows, heart, and rainbow.*

Waves lash on shores
*   red spruce bends and bows,*
*   jabbing heaviness.*

Sunshine amidst blue-
  skied clouds

Daffodil heads hang
  pansies weeping in pots.

April showers
  marshal

May flowers

We rise again.

  with thanks to the Rankin Family

In a Moment

everything can change . . .

Be. The. Change.

love all peoples

today.

Acknowledgments

With gratitude and thanks to The Muse.

My children and grandchildren, with special thanks to my oldest grandson, Theo, for gracing this book with his marvelous photos.

Gretchen Jones, who first told me that my writing was given to be shared, Jeanne L. Thompson who pushed me not too gently into a writing life.

Doris Jakobsh, Brenda Jewitt, Jane Walker, Laurie Wilkinson, and so many others, you know who you are, who edit, offer support and listen to me over and over again.

Lindy Mechefske who edited this work with encouragement and honesty.

Daniel Crack who has exhibited patience, creativity and flexibility as he listened to me every step of the way in the publication of this collection.

Liw and Susan who have lived through the days of this pandemic supporting, loving and encouraging me. I could not have written these words without you.

Thank you each one.

www.ingramcontent.com/pod-product-compliance
Lightning Source LLC
Chambersburg PA
CBHW021451070526
44577CB00002B/364